Show Ponies and Workhorses

SALES ENGINEERING IN THE
TELECOMMUNICATIONS CIRCUS

DAN PITTS

Contents

Forward 3
    Background 3
    Purpose 4

Chapter 1 -- What is an SE? 7
    Definition of an Engineer 8
    Knowing the Theory 9
    Engineer vs. Technician 10
    Critical Thinking 13
    Requirements 14

Chapter 2 -- Discipline of Sales 19
    Customer Focus 20
    Customer Relationship 23
    Capital "S", Capital "E" 25

Chapter 3 -- The Show Pony and the Workhorse 29
    The Sales Team 30
        Role of Sales 30
        Role of SE 33
        Reality of Role 38
    Ideal Relationship 44

Chapter 4 -- Customer Relationships 47
    Commercial vs. Technical 47
    Value of Technical Relationships 48
    Customer Meetings and Travel 52

Chapter 5 -- Building and Maintaining Knowledge 54
    Running with Scissors 56

Chapter 6 -- Developing Expertise – Building Personal Brand ...59
- Attitude 59
- Commitment 60
- Drive 61
- Process 64
- Technology 67
- Communication 67

Chapter 7 -- Time Management 71
- Multitasking 71
- Prioritization 74
- Agenda 76

Chapter 8 -- Issues and Resolution 79
- The Difficult Sales Director 79
- Organizational Power 81
- Competing Priorities 84
- Work Overload 85
- Unrealistic Expectations 86
- The Difficult Customer 87

Chapter 9 -- Why I was an SE 89
- Final Thoughts 90

Works Cited 91

Forward

Background

I have been a Sales Engineer or a Sales Engineering Manager over the past fifteen years and recognize that there is a gap in training and advice specifically targeted for Sales Engineers. The bulk of training revolves around the discipline of Sales, and while it is important, it does not fully prepare SEs for the role. Sales Engineering is a stand-alone discipline. It has grown out of "technical sales" and is closely related to Sales, but requires a unique skill set and can be leveraged to increase sales productivity. This book is targeted at the Sales Engineer or SE to provide advice both on the actual role, but also on how the role fits within the organization. Much of the advice contained comes from addressing real world situations with various customers and internal organizations throughout my career. Often, the SE is treated somewhat like a "second class citizen" or "support" on the Sales team. If there is training geared for the SEs, it typically revolves around the technology that is offered as part of any solutions sold. What is missing are the soft skills such as how to identify and develop technical contacts, or how to leverage total cost of ownership in solutions to drive value. The following lays out a framework for the soft skill topics that are directly relevant to the SE. As customer demands become more complex, the need for SEs will increase in Sales organizations. My intention is to provide a compilation of advice to serve as a guide for new SEs as well as provide some clarity around the role of SE for both Sales and SEs that will help technical sales teams become more effective and drive revenue.

Purpose

So many books have been written on Sales, yet relatively few address the role of the Sales Engineer. In a "highly scientific" experiment, aka Google search, a search for "books on sales engineering" yielded 2.55M returns, while "books on sales x" with the x being found in the following table with associated results:

Strategy	49.5M
Prospecting	0.5M
Management	14.9M
Leadership	2.74M
Operations	7.8M

My conclusion? Sales Engineering is obviously closely related to Sales Leadership. So, perhaps this is not the case, but it is a fun comparison. Honestly, Sales Engineering is an area of critical importance to Sales, especially Technical Sales, but is often regarded as a support role or a role that is used as a stepping stone to Sales. Sales Engineering should be viewed as its own discipline with its own set of metrics and organizational structure. Typically, the Sales Engineering organization will have its own management structure, but will be subordinate either to Sales or a Sales support organization. Is this going to change over time? Is the SE going to become the heroic savior of the corporate world? No. The reality is that Sales is and always will be the driver of the organization because this is the revenue engine that makes the company work. Companies make fundamental changes to Sales and Revenue at high risk, therefore it is unlikely for any paradigm shifts to take place within the Sales organization.

The purpose of this book is to provide lessons learned over more than fifteen years of experience in Sales Engineering to provide a productive path for collaborating with Sales to drive revenue. The goal is not to replace Sales or take on a more important role from Sales, rather to provide suggestions for working more effectively with Sales. Organizations that could improve performance view the Sales Engineer as a support role that takes direction from Sales. The best organizations consider the Sales Engineer to be a fully participating team member or partner with Sales.

Show Ponies and Workhorses

Chapter 1 -- What is an SE?

An SE is a Sales Engineer or a Solutions Engineer that is typically working in a technical industry such as communications, software or networking to sell services or products. Throughout my career, I have sold Telecommunications, Internet, Broadcast Video and Satellite Networking solutions. Some other key industries include but are not limited to software, security and network hardware. Typically, the product or service being sold is technically complex and is continually evolving. There is a requirement for "someone" to understand how the product or service actually works, what the benefit of the product or service is to the prospective customer and be able to convey this in layman's terms.

For example, we now have Satellites that can provide over - 20dB Carrier/Noise to locations within the footprint of a beam, which enables a satellite modem to transmit a carrier at modulations of up to 256APSK. Are you kidding me? What does this even mean? In this example, the role of the SE is to explain to the customer that if s/he upgrades their modem to a new one capable of this modulation and moves to the new satellite capacity, they can increase the amount of bandwidth transmitted over 10MHz of satellite capacity from 20Mbps to 50Mbps, and by the way, we will gladly sell you the modem. The point is, who cares about technological innovation unless you can translate it into a business case for the customer? In this case, the customer typically buys the satellite capacity in MHz so that they can resell or use it for something useful like transmitting Internet access over it. The SE needs to sell the concept to the decision-maker, the one writing the checks. Of course it is important to get buy-in from the customer's technical experts, but the real sale is with the check writer. It is critical to be able to translate technical capability into business advantage.

Definition of an Engineer

What is an Engineer? While the obsolete definition is a "crafty schemer", an engineer is defined as "a person who is trained in or follows as a profession a branch of engineering" or "a person who carries through an enterprise by skillful or artful contrivance". (Merriam-Webster Online Dictionary, 2017) While Sales Engineering is not a classical engineering branch such as Mechanical, Electrical, Chemical or Civil Engineering, it truly is a blend of several disciplines depending on what you are selling. To develop terrestrial network solutions, there is a combination of Electrical Engineering through IP networking, optical networking and power delivery to gear, while elements of Mechanical Engineering are used to allocate for HVAC requirements and heat dissipation in data centers or colocation facilities. The point is that the term "Engineer" should not be viewed as simply a title tacked on to the end of a job description. The reason universities do not hand out Bachelor of Engineering degrees without the completion of a rigorous four year program of hell is that it is truly a profession and there are some baseline skills acquired in any engineering program. The main skill is learning how to think critically. Engineers are problem solvers and have learned how to break down large problems into smaller issues and solve in discrete elements.

Knowing the Theory

I cannot emphasize strongly enough the importance of really learning and understanding the theory behind whatever you are selling. If you selling terrestrial networks, then you must know the OSI stack inside and out and understand the IP protocol at the packet level. Know the bits that comprise the header for all of the protocols used – IP, MPLS, Ethernet, Optical, etc. Really learn the routing protocols and how they work. The theory is the key to all services developed as it is the technology used to enable services. If you are selling satellite networks, you must become an expert on RF theory, which is the physics of isotropic radiation. If you are selling software, then you must know how to code and have a deep understanding of the software that has been developed.

Why is being an expert on the underlying theory of your product and/or service so important? Not only does this knowledge provide you with a high level of credibility with your customers, it also insulates you against the development of new technologies that are adopted as services. If you are a "One Trick Pony" and know all of the mechanics of Layer 3 routing, for example, you may have issues if a new technology such as Optical or Layer 1 networking is adopted. Being grounded in the theory enables you to flexibly adapt to any technologies based on the theory. You are an Engineer, not a Technician.

Where can I learn the theory? Think textbooks, like college course textbooks. For example, a great resource for the theory on the IP Protocol can be found in <u>Internetworking with TCP/IP Volume One</u> by Douglas Comer. This is a textbook that thoroughly breaks down the IP protocol in an in-depth manner and I highly recommend this to anyone developing solutions that use the IP protocol. An example of a good source for Satellite networking is <u>Satellite Communications</u> by Timothy Pratt and Charles Bostian. Again, this is a textbook that thoroughly covers the theory behind the services. The point is that you need to understand the technology as an engineer so that you can play with the concepts to develop solutions for a wide variety of requirements.

Engineer vs. Technician

Earlier, I described the ability of the engineer to break a problem down into discrete elements. So how can you break down a solution into defined chunks? You have to focus on the customer requirements. Engineers are trained to capture and address true requirements. Further, by working with the underlying theory of the technical solution, new innovative solutions and approaches can be offered or at least considered. There is a huge difference between an engineer and a technician. A technician will have an understanding of the tasks required to complete a solution, but often the tasks are based on a particular technology. For example, in IP Networking, a technician may know all of the commands and intimate details for configuring a router, or even more specifically a Cisco or Juniper router. The technician will likely be a "Go To guy" for any routing or Layer 3 issues and will be able to engineer solutions as long as it falls within this technology (IP routing). When a new technology is introduced such as Optical or Layer 1 networking, the Layer 3 knowledge is not as useful which will lead to a few issues. 1) the technician will be resistant to the change because it is a new technology that will require training and study and 2) the technician will attempt to solve problems with the older technology (Layer 3) framework. The engineer, on the other hand, by knowing the theory of packet networks will understand that we are simply changing the packets from a Layer 3 to a Layer 1 protocol and will work to learn the nomenclature and configuration of the new Layer 1 technology. The theory will have the same underlying principals but the methods and process will change, because new gear will be used. This will lead to changes in solutions and may identify opportunities for improvement.

Are there examples of technicians that become "Super Engineers"? Of course, but the majority of technicians are very much wed to what they have learned in the past. So what does this mean? If you find yourself in a Sales Engineering role without an engineering degree, is it over? Do you need to dust off the resume? Absolutely not. The key is to understand the real value of an engineering degree which is to learn "How to learn the **theory** of a subject" and be able to apply it to solve problems. If you have not taken engineering courses at a university, then look into enrolling into a few within your discipline. There are several universities that offer online courses and you will likely be able to receive tuition assistance from your employer. The goal of taking any of these courses is to "learn how to learn". Pay attention to how the theory is derived, typically from a Law of Physics (at least this is the case in Mechanical Engineering), then learn how to apply it to everyday problems. You need to understand why a solution will work from a theoretical standpoint. Once you have this concept, you will be able to flexibly adapt to technology surrounding the solution as it changes because the theory will not.

Critical Thinking

So if you are going to use the word "Engineer" on your business card, then you need to have the proper mindset. The most important trait of an Engineer is the ability to think critically. So what is critical thinking? Below is a definition from The Critical Thinking Community:

> Critical thinking is that mode of thinking — about any subject, content, or problem — in which the thinker improves the quality of his or her thinking by skillfully analyzing, assessing, and reconstructing it. Critical thinking is self-directed, self-disciplined, self-monitored, and self-corrective thinking. It presupposes assent to rigorous standards of excellence and mindful command of their use. It entails effective communication and problem-solving abilities, as well as a commitment to overcome our native egocentrism and sociocentrism. (Our Concept and Definition of Critical Thinking, 2017)

Well, I am not so concerned with overcoming egocentrism or sociocentrism, but the self-motivated analysis and objective conclusion is what I am talking about. When a customer is looking for a solution that s/he will actually pay for, there should be more than enough motivation to figure out how to make it happen. Typically, products or services offered may need to be tweaked a bit in order to truly address the customer requirements, otherwise, they would buy services online or in some pre-packaged format that does not require much interaction. The challenge is to develop a solution that will work for the customer without causing a huge issue with Operations to implement and maintain the solution. This takes **critical thinking**.

Requirements

Capturing accurate and proper requirements from the customer is a key function of the SE. It truly is important to be able to differentiate a "want" from a requirement. A want is a characteristic of the solution but is not a make or break item that will kill the deal if it is not met. A requirement must be met in order for the solution to be viable. As an SE, you will deal with a lot of customers that will insist that their wants are requirements. The trick is to clearly lay out the requirements for a solution and obtain concurrence with your customer. It is OK to iterate on this subject until you arrive at agreement. Get this agreement first before spending hours on a solution. If not, you can create the most beautiful solution only to find out a key requirement has not been met, killing the deal. Of course, at this point, you not only get to deal with both your and the customer's disappointment, but also the gentle and accommodating understanding of Sales.

An example conversation may go something like this, "I need to build a network to serve Internet Access to cruise ships providing a minimum of 100Mbps for receive traffic and a minimum of 50Mbps for transmit traffic from each ship. The solution must use the existing gear deployed on the ships today and be priced at a 20% discount to what is in place. " So what are the requirements in this simple request?

The requirement is to develop a network that can provide 100 x 50 Mbps per ship. Period. If you can develop the solution that uses the existing gear and decreases the cost 20%, awesome, but if this were so easy to accomplish, why doesn't the customer simply ask for an incremental component to what they already have? Break the problem down into its components and solve for primary and alternative solutions. What solution can provide a 100 x 50 Mbps network? What gear can be used to provide this network, does it really have to use the existing gear? No. The existing gear should be one of the options, but the overall total cost of ownership may change with different gear and solutions. Finally, is the cost decrease of 20% a requirement? Hardly. This is where the "Sales" in Sales Engineering comes into play. You need to define the tradeoffs between the cost and the capabilities of your solutions. If you can develop a solution that requires new gear but is capable of serving 100 x 50 Mbps for multiple ships on the same network, what is the overall total cost of ownership for the fleet of ships for this solution? How does this compare to the existing solution? Is there benefit, possibly enough benefit to increase the price for the solution, but replace the existing solution with a more cost effective total solution for the customer? My point is, the more you can expand solutions into overall capabilities for the customer, the more variables you have to work with to craft better performance and cost effectiveness. Try not to get boxed into a corner on a specific solution and price. Work to develop "total cost of ownership" models. This may include the cost of capital for new gear, the OPEX or operational expense to manage the gear, and the amount of service required to be purchased to run on the gear. When expanding the solution into this broader context, there are more components to tweak to arrive at an optimal solution.

Price is easy to compare, especially when comparing "apples to apples". For solutions, it is often difficult to compare in an "apples to apples" fashion because if they are broad enough, there are too many variables. If you are working as an SE, then the product or service you are selling is sufficiently complex to require a technical expert to complete the sale. You do not see a gang of SEs hanging out at Walmart developing solutions for a collection of products. The products are pretty self-explanatory, and people pretty much know what they want at

Walmart. For software, security or networking solutions, SEs are pretty common because solutions need to be developed to align with the services sold and technology is continually changing which forces updates to existing services.

So this is directly at odds with "Purchasing Gone Wild". There is certainly a movement within purchasing departments today to break down services into RFPs and comparison spreadsheets in order to compare the costs of solutions on an "apples to apples" basis. In other words, the purchasing department is looking to boil everything in a solution down to a commodity, then price on a $/unit basis of that commodity. Try as much as possible to counter this type of request or RFP with a Total Cost of Ownership offering. The problem with adhering to the cost spreadsheet demanded by purchasing is that the only comparison is the price and the solutions can be wildly different. Again, this is where the Sales hat needs to be worn and negotiations with the customer are required to arrive at defined requirements. Trust me, the ability to convince the customer of the value of your solution, even when it does not exactly address what the customer has asked for (but does satisfy the requirements) takes critical thinking.

Show Ponies and Workhorses

Chapter 2 -- Discipline of Sales

Before I moved into Sales Engineering, I had some opinions concerning Sales. These opinions were formed based on the behavior of Sales individuals I knew and drew the conclusion that it seemed like it was easy, Sales had a lot of fun and made a ton of money. What's not to like and why isn't everyone doing this? Well, there are plenty of Sales folks that are successful, make a lot of money and do have some fun, but "it ain't easy". Sales truly is a discipline that must be learned to excel. Most of the focus surrounds building relationships and learning how to interact with customers as well as senior management. The role of Sales is to essentially become a student of the customer's organization and build relationships with the key players that purchase stuff, especially the stuff you are selling. Much of this discipline involves learning the organization of the customer and identifying the relationship with the key players. Are they supporters of your organization, are they indifferent or do they just hate you? Learning this helps to set strategies to either change opinions or learn the "path" that will be required to approve a project and win a sale.

The most important information to obtain from your customers is to learn where their strategy is taking them and what initiatives are being launched. Learning how to obtain this information and apply solutions to customer initiatives is the core discipline of Sales.

Customer Focus

We always hear about the importance of customer focus. What does this really mean? In industries that use Sales Engineers, the product or service is typically technically complex and the pool of customers is fairly focused. Often, solutions are built in a wholesale fashion for customers that resell service to end customers such as general consumers. The key to customer focus is to "live" in your customer's world and develop strategies that will drive revenue in those markets. What are your customer's products and services? How are they performing financially? Who are their competitors? What are substitutes to your customer's products and services? How can your product or service help to drive revenue for your customer?

Where do you draw the line with customer focus? Well, one way of helping the bottom line or Net Income for a company is to increase the revenue obtained. Another way is to reduce the cost of sales. Your focus must be on increasing the revenue and not "giving away the farm" by reducing the price of your product/service and reducing the cost of sales. Your contacts at the customer will want to focus on reducing the cost of sales and will put pressure on your offerings. The reason for this is that typically the organization you are working with at the customer is not in Sales and do not have metrics for performance tied to revenue. If you are selling a technically complex solution, you will likely be working with an Operations, Engineering or Product team responsible for rolling out a new product or service. Their goals and metrics will be tied to deployment timelines as well as cost control. You need to identify the owner of the initiative and be able to discuss the overall business case associated with the initiative and your product/service to illustrate how revenue can be increased rather than the cost of your solution. To be credible, you really need to know your customer's business and build a relationship with a key influencer within the organization to work with you on a solution and champion it through the approval process.

Isn't this obvious? Well, the activities I am describing are more strategic activities that require some thought and planning. Often, Sales runs at a frenetic pace, focusing on "customer issues" that arise randomly throughout the week or day even. In the drive to remain customer focused, Sales will immediately jump on issues that arise from the customer. An example issue may be receiving an email or phone call stating that they customer is receiving lower than expected performance of an existing solution. This will often turn into hours if not a day or two of collecting data, researching the issue and either fixing the issue or proving that the solution is working as expected. While this is necessary, it is a tactical reaction to customer driven events. Most of your time will be spent on tactical issues, either working to develop an opportunity or reacting to customer issues or even self-imposed issues within your own organization. I am not saying that these issues should be ignored, but you need to ensure that time is set aside for strategic activities such as developing business cases for your solutions that focus on driving revenue for your customer.

Really, the only way to figure out what initiatives the customer is developing or what direction the customer is heading is through the establishment of enough constant contact that you can ask probing questions and learn how to best apply your services toward their goal. You must think strategically about your customer's business to enable these sorts of discussions. Perhaps you set up monthly "Ops Reviews" or "Health Status" meetings to get feedback on performance. The real reason you are there is to elicit requirements from initiatives. If you are not thinking strategically and only reacting to customer complaints or requests, you will never get there. Set aside the time to develop a communication strategy as part of an account plan for each of your customers. As an SE, you should develop a "Technical Account Plan". This could be a simple inventory of overall services your customer has purchased and a comparison of what you have sold the customer as a percentage of their overall spend. What technologies are used? Are they old, is there a better answer? Are there any initiatives or drivers that may require a new architecture or model? How can your customer more efficiently drive revenue? Is there any innovation that can be applied to provide a better product or service from your customer? Notice, that I am not looking to marry up any product or service from your company in these questions. The key element to answer is how can my customer drive revenue? If you can clearly answer this AND tie a solution together with your products and services, then beautiful. If not, then some innovation within your company may be required. Are your competitors able to offer a solution? The point is that you need to bring value to the relationship. Providing insight is valuable, even if you do not have a direct service that can offer a solution. You are building the relationship; your time will come.

Customer Relationship

The customer relationship is everything. If a service requires an SE, then the relationship with the customer should not be transactional. SEs do not sell "widgets", and the product is not made in a factory. I cannot emphasize enough that SEs provide services. Products are made in factories and basically are a "thing" in which ownership is passed. A factory creates the product (like a bar of soap), packages it, where it is transported to a store and sold to a consumer that then owns it. Even in the network hardware industry, where actual products like router or platform chassis and cards are sold, the focus tends to revolve around the "service" of licensing the software and the maintenance agreement.

SEs sell services, whether it is a software suite with a maintenance contract or an MPLS network. The key difference between a product and service is that the service is typically owned by a company that then leases or licenses the use of the service to the customer, typically paid in periodic payments. The ownership of a product is transferred at sale to the consumer and is typically purchased once.

I actually worked at a telecommunications provider that insisted on calling their Operations Department "the factory" and had an entire department of "Product Management". I am here to tell you that no telecommunication provider is selling a product, except if they want to sell stand-alone routers or other network gear. Typically, telecommunication providers are looking to sell circuits or a network of some sort that may or may not include network gear that is paid for each month until the contract term expires. This, my friends is a service and is why the SE is integral. Someone has got to develop the design of the network for the customer, which is usually the customer's Network Engineering team. There are a wide variety of options to move bits from customer locations to datacenters for example. Determining a compelling path is the role of the SE. So, what is "compelling"? New technologies and price points can lead to different architectures. If a customer has a network in place for several years, there may be new designs that can be applied to extract more performance at or near the same cost, possibly even less. This is compelling.

The components of the networks are typically standardized, but each customer implementation is unique. In order to effectively develop the network, a clear understanding of customer requirements, drivers and initiatives is paramount. The only way to obtain this information is to build an excellent customer relationship. How else are you going to learn about the potential for upgrades or expansions?

Capital "S", Capital "E"

The goal of an SE is to perform such that you are viewed as a Capital "S", Capital "E". That is, you are very strong in both Sales and Engineering. They are two separate disciplines. Be a student of both and learn to excel at both. There are numerous Sales trainings that are available. Learn how to categorize key personnel within your customer's organization. Map out the approval chain of your customer. Often this is not aligned according to the organization chart. Map out the inventory of services that the customer has today and what services may be needed to address initiatives. In order to become a Capital "S", you must conduct activities that no one is going to explicitly task you. You may be asked to create an account plan, but this is likely assigned to Sales as a deliverable within their management chain. You may be included in developing the account plan, often you are not because SE is frequently considered "Sales Support". This truly is a moniker that makes me bristle. An SE should be considered an equal part of the Sales Team. In order to be treated as an equal partner, you must act and perform like an equal partner and "bring something to the table". Learn various sales techniques, take a negotiation class or two, and set goals for every interaction with your customer. In essence you must learn and take on the Sales Role, but your focus should be on influencing the technical organization of your customer.

While you are learning sales techniques and aligning them with the preferred methodology of your Sales team, you must also be viewed as a Capital "E". That is, you could easily work in the core engineering group of your company developing new products or services. You must have an in-depth knowledge of your service and genuinely have interest in specifications and capabilities of key components that are used to provide the service. The knowledge must come from a deep theoretical understanding overlaid with experience. Be a student of the technology or discipline that drives your service. For example, if you are selling communication services, you must become an expert in the IP networking protocol and theory. You should also be an expert on the gear used to provide the service and clearly be able to outline the capabilities and limitations of various solutions. The change in the industry is rapid, therefore, you must stay abreast of new technologies and protocols that enable more cost effective solutions. You have to be an enthusiastic student of the discipline. If you are "going through the motions" or remain stagnant with your knowledge of the underlying technology, your solutions will reflect this and will not stand out to your customer. Even if the customer is not quite ready for new technologies and solutions, it is always insightful to receive an option or proposal that incorporates new capabilities to expose your customer to the possibilities the new technology may bring. This also cements your position with the customer as bringing value and working your way to being a "trusted advisor". Of course, this is more work than simply addressing stated requirements with a solution, but Sales is a competitive game and you must set yourself apart.

Note that an SE is not a Network Engineer or functional engineer. The main goal is to drive revenue by selling solutions.

Show Ponies and Workhorses

This means that the best solution is the one that the customer will buy, and it may not necessarily be the most cost effective or technically outstanding. The solution that is purchased IS the best solution, at least for the customer that buys it. A clear understanding of the customer's budget and price expectations are key to developing a winning solution. Work closely with Sales to determine these parameters. Develop multiple solutions as options, but one solution MUST meet the budget requirements. Finally, do not get technical "religion" on various technologies. If a customer insists on using a technology that is clearly inferior to established technologies, it is certainly worth discussing the pros and cons of both technologies with your customer. After such a discussion, it is important, however, to go with the customer's technology decision no matter how insane the decision may be. Do not try to convince the customer that they are wrong or that they need to convert to your technology – this will not end well. As an SE, you have performed your duty by exposing the customer to technology that may be better, but if the customer sticks with "their" technology, then so be it. Remember, the best solution is the one that the customer buys.

Chapter 3 -- The Show Pony and the Workhorse

There is an old joke that describes the members of a Sales Team. The analogy is that the Sales people are "Show Ponies". They are dolled up, dance around the ring and receive all of the attention. So pretty. On the other hand, the SEs are more like workhorses or Clydesdales. You know, the team of horses that pull the enormous Budweiser truck, or the ones that actually are used to plow a field. It is a humorous analogy but is actually quite relevant. Sales is responsible for building and maintaining relationships on the account. They must be engaging, have strong rapport and be able to attract the attention of their customers. Attractiveness is a good trait in this area. The SE is the "brains" of the operation. They must convey the confidence of a technical expert, and are typically viewed as a partner or even "side kick" to the Sales representative, or "star". When I say sidekick, I do not mean a clown like Sideshow Bob to Crusty the Clown in the Simpsons, but rather Goose to Maverick in TopGun. In a strong Sales Team, the sum is always greater than the parts.

Show Ponies and Workhorses

The Sales Team

The Sales Team should be comprised of a Sales professional (Account Director, Sales Director, Account Representative, etc.) and an SE (Sales Engineer, Systems Engineer, Solutions Architect, etc.). Often the SE will be spread across multiple Sales team members within an organization. In this case, the SE must view each relationship as a team. They will all have different strengths and weaknesses and the SE must be flexible to adapt styles and roles depending the strengths of the Sales team member and the relationship established with the customer. The best way to establish a strong team and clearly define roles and responsibilities on the team is to have constant communication within the team. As an SE, you should have daily interaction with the Sales team member, no matter how many teammates you have. If you do not establish this communication and act as a team member and align goals, then you will be treated as simply support to sales and will be given tasks to complete instead of working as a team.

Role of Sales

Sales will always take the lead on a customer engagement and will always assume that they are in charge and will make the decisions. This is by design. Sales is given a quota to sell a given amount of business and it is up to the Sales team member to figure out how to exceed the quota. There are infinite ways that Sales can attack this responsibility. Some choose to handle everything themselves, often with little to no regard for internal organizations, process or delivery timelines. Others are very collaborative, play by the "rules" or internal processes, and many are a mix of the two. The key point is that "the business" (senior management, finance, etc.) does not really care how it is achieved as long as revenue targets are being met. Of course, Senior Management will always prefer to have the organization running smoothly where all of the internal organizations work together to exceed performance goals. Senior Management, however, will tolerate the type of Sales person that stresses the organization through escalations and out of process behavior and promises as long as the revenue objectives are being met or exceeded. This is especially true in a public company where reporting is performed every quarter. If revenue objectives are not being met, then the "problem child" will likely be replaced.

The role of Sales is to contract for as much revenue as possible. The overall revenue that a company has forecast for a given period is then allocated to the Sales teams for individual responsibility. Sales must then figure out how the revenue assigned will be achieved. If the revenue is achieved, typically the pay is enough to motivate Sales to continue this process for the next period. If the revenue is not achieved, pay typically is significantly reduced which may lead to the loss of motivation for the next period resulting in the movement to another job, or the Sales team member may be asked to leave due to performance. Sales professionals that stay with the same company for a long time have typically figured out how to exceed their quota period after period. Therefore, the main focus for Sales is how they are performing according to THEIR quota. How this is achieved is secondary, the impact of a deal on the company is secondary, increased workload or out of process implementation is secondary to the achievement of quota. Sales personnel are hired for this focus because revenue growth is difficult to obtain and an organization needs a team with their sole focus on revenue. The argument of changing a deal for the "good of the company" or boosting a metric other than revenue such as yield or margin is going to fall on deaf ears if it does not promote revenue. The only way to make a change is to change the metrics that Sales are measured against. That is, the measure that they are paid commission. If revenue achievement is changed to margin attainment for overall deals, then margin will become the focus. The key point is that Sales is geared to act in their self-interest according to the metrics set before them. They are motivated to make money by achieving their targets and are hired to do so. Sales will act in the best interest of the company as long as this is aligned properly with their quota.

Role of SE

So what is the key role of the SE on the Sales team? The SE is the only engineering group in the company that has a focus on driving revenue. While revenue is the key driver, it does not mean that the SE leads the engagement with the customer on pricing. This is the Sales role. It is truly important to understand the roles and responsibilities within the Sales Team. Just as you would not expect the Sales Director to fully design and develop solutions, the SE should not be developing the pitch to the customer. The most effective pitches and solutions come from a very collaborative effort between the Sales Director and the SE. The key is that you do not want to cross too far over into areas of expertise, otherwise there becomes a questioning of value of the other team member. The role of the SE is to capture the true customer requirements, identify customer initiatives for strategic projects and to develop solutions leveraging components your company can provide to address these needs. Often, through considerable experience, the SE will have a deep understanding of what will or will not work concerning cost for a customer, especially one in a long-standing relationship. This knowledge should be used as a factor to develop the pitch for any new solutions that will be proposed. The key item, however, is that the Sales Director must develop the pitch as there are many factors that drive the development of the pitch that are outside of the solution.

Show Ponies and Workhorses

Sales is responsible for revenue attainment; their livelihood is dependent on it. Sales either attains quota and receives commission or they do not. Sales will behave according to their incentives, which is what is expected. So, if Sales is incented to drive revenue, prices may fall and margin may not be great, but revenue will be achieved. If margin is paramount, then less revenue will likely be achieved as only those deals with favorable margin will be won. It really depends on the business cycle of the company as to what metrics are used for Sales.

For the most part, SEs are typically spread across a few to many Sales Directors, depending on the complexity of the sale. This means that the SE has more of an average revenue attainment or quota. The result is that the commission is fairly predictable, but there are no wild swings either up or down. The analogy has been used that the SE commission is more like a mutual fund whereas the Sales commission is more like an individual stock. The SE should develop the right solution to fit the pricing required to get the deal. For example, if your customer insists on only buying the lowest priced offers and treats you like a vendor, then do not "gold plate" the design. Develop a solution that minimally addresses the requirements. If you are working with a true partner where you have a great relationship, then go out of your way to overachieve with your design – treat it as your own company. The result of the great design will lead to more business, especially with a partner. Providing more value than necessary to a price-focused customer will not likely lead to additional business. Those customers in the "vendor" relationship only come back in search of cheap pricing – so give them what they want.

Again, what is the role of the SE? Of course, it depends on the organization and the metrics set for SE performance. Some organizations pay commission to SEs like Sales, others pay a bonus like the majority of non-Sales employees. Even if the SE is paid commission, the performance is typically measured across multiple accounts or Sales leads as SEs are not typically assigned to a single account or Sales Lead. So what is the point of this discussion on commission and bonus? Well, if the SE is tied to bonus, then the SE should be motivated to perform in a manner to maximize their bonus. For example, if a significant portion of a bonus is tied to EBITDA performance of the company, then the SE should help steer deals to maximize EBITDA. If you are unfamiliar with what is driving your bonus, then do some homework so that you understand the measure of performance and learn what drives the metric. You should act to maximize that metric. This may be somewhat shocking to the Sales Director, especially if it creates another constraint on a deal. In this example, I mean that pure revenue may not be good for EBITDA, **profitable** revenue will.

Show Ponies and Workhorses

The bottom line is that in general, the SE should have more of a "company benefit" focus. Selling a deal is great and the goal of the work, but selling a "bad" deal can cause damage to the company. Be wary of chasing revenue by lowering prices to the point, where there is no margin or negative margin on the deal. If you lose a dollar for every widget you sell, you cannot make up for the gap by selling more volume. While this is simplistic and somewhat common sense, the number of deals that get signed that break this rule are numerous. Why? You are still getting revenue which is typically the metric for Sales. So, one role is to be the honest broker on the team and work to keep the best interests of the company in mind. Another role is to maximize the metrics of your pay plan. If this pay plan is in complete lockstep with Sales, then there should be zero friction as a team -- go close deals and chase revenue. If your metrics are aligned with margin and Sales is driven by revenue, then there may be some friction, but the bottom line is that Sales will make more revenue when closing deals with excellent margin. If deals are cutting into margin and have a detrimental effect on your metrics, then more collaboration is required. You do not want to be viewed as a lackey that agrees to everything the Sales Director directs and follows blindly. The Sales/SE relationship should be a partnership.

Of course, the other component of the SE role is to be the technical expert on the team. If you are constantly answering customer questions in a meeting with, "Good question, I will check with (our experts) on that and get back to you next week", what in the Hell are you doing in the meeting? Learn the technology inside and out. Be an expert on customer solutions with this technology. Know your subject matter and be authoritative in meetings. Question your customers to derive requirements. The only way to find out the true requirements are to ask questions. Typically, your customers are not as well versed on your technology, why else would they come to you? Be the expert and most importantly, **convey confidence**. If your statement concerning your solution seems like a question or if there is the slightest hesitation, you have just opened the game of "20 questions". The customer will lose confidence in your solution and will ask an untold number of questions in order to determine if they have confidence in your solution. It is far better to go in guns blazing with confidence with an 80% correct solution, than it is to meekly suggest a solution that is absolutely 100% correct. If there are issues with the solution, then address them quickly and move on, with confidence. The reality is that you are likely the only one who knows the difference between the 80% and 100% solution. Explaining caveats or possibilities how a solution may fall apart only detract from your message. Go into your meeting or communication with the customer about your solution as enthusiastic and positive as possible. Solve for the 80% solution for a quick response, and deliver a confident message. Of course, tweaks may be required down the road, but the point is that you are responsive and authoritative. This will build your relationship with the customer, as well as the Sales Lead.

Finally, you own the technical solution. Accept this responsibility and drive it to conclusion. Sales Leads may have input, but you have the final say and need to drive it within the organization and the account. This is sacred, treat it like Sales treats pricing.

Reality of Role

The reality of the SE role is that you are the workhorse. No one dresses up the workhorse and parades it around the stadium for its beauty, except for maybe Clydesdales, but then they are typically hauling beer. Accept the role as partner, sidekick, co-pilot, etc. There typically is no glory in the position, but you are an important piece of the Sales team. Further, the SE is a much more stable position than Sales. You are the technical interface to the customer. This is not something learned overnight as you not only become an expert on the technology but also build relationships with the customers and learn their behavior. Missing revenue targets are not directly attributable to your performance, this is more of a Sales focus. Of course, if you consistently miss revenue targets over time, there is going to be a problem. One of the larger issues that I was able to bypass by being an SE is that I did not have to close the deal. By this, I mean that I did not have chase the customer day after day, hour after hour to get them to sign the deal in order to meet an end of month or end of quarter deadline. I liked to be in the Sales Organization, but the badgering often required to close deals did not align with my skill set. Often, SEs question whether they should be in Sales. While it is very similar, there are certain traits that enable Sales Directors to excel. You must examine whether you have these traits and if you have the proper mindset. Anyone can sell, but those that excel tend to have more self-interest, are able to engage virtually anyone in an interesting manner and like to be the star of the show. Usually, SEs do not just wake up in their role. There is an active decision to go into the field and the reason is more often than not influenced by personality factors. If the SE is truly geared for Sales, then they would already be there given their need to be the star of the show. Of course, there are plenty of former SEs in Sales. They tend to make excellent Sales Directors and value the role of the SE, but just because you are an effective SE, does not mean you will excel in Sales. Again, they are two different disciplines.

Show Ponies and Workhorses

Recognition and Workload

So if the SE does not receive the big commission checks, then the draw to be an SE must be in the constant recognition from the company and adulation from peers, right? Perhaps not. SEs will typically have a few "spots" in the end of year awards, such as a President's Club trip or other Sales awards, but the ratio is much less than Sales. For example, Sales will typically award recipients for every Department within Sales. If several Departments combine to form a Region, the typical SE winner will be awarded for the Region, not the Department level. While it is nice to receive recognition for performance, do not expect it as an SE. You will receive a lot of verbal recognition from the Sales award winners as they are accepting their award that "owe it all to the SE", but they are not going to share the award check. If you are looking for the company recognition such as a President's Club trip or company awards, keep in mind that these are mainly geared for Sales as way to incent their top performers so that they do not jump ship to competitors. Also keep in mind that Sales tends to be a much more transient field that Sales Engineering. Remember, SEs are the workhorses not the Show Ponies. I know that some critics will read this and claim that this is just the jaded perception of a has-been SE that never received any recognition. (Fighting through bitter tears) It is true that I never did receive the President's Club trips or anything resembling an 'SE of the Year' award. My point is that upon reflection, it is somewhat surprising that any awards are given to SEs. I certainly was not performing in order to receive an award, and really never expected one. It would be nice to receive one, but to expect one is only setting yourself up for disappointment – even when your Sales Director receives an award. I believe that SEs are given awards to illustrate that the company values the performance of the SE and at least accepts the partnership concept. The real reason for the Sales awards is to retain top Sales performers and the flight risk of SEs to the competition is not the same as Sales. Therefore, the awards will not be commensurate with Sales and any award should be received with an incredulous grin.

Well, if the recognition is not the same as Sales, then the workload must be more manageable, correct? Sure. Think about it, if you are assigned to multiple Sales Directors, your workload is being driven by multiple Sales Directors. Typically, there are periods of feast and famine when it comes to workload. It depends on how active your accounts become. Therefore it is critical to be able to focus and prioritize. You must be able to produce an excellent product the first time within a tight time constraint, and then move onto the next project with the same focus. Further, you must have a great dialogue with all your Sales Directors so that you set proper expectations for them as to when solutions will be completed.

Show Ponies and Workhorses

Of course, prioritization must be applied, otherwise you will produce mediocre results for all of your projects. The key to keeping your workload under control is to be in constant contact with your Sales Directors. Meet with them daily, get a feel for their priorities and assess what deals are near closing. Focus on your metrics to set priorities. One thing is for certain, you will always have more tasks due than you can perform in a day. Develop a strategy for handling your tasks. You may want to refer to the Time Management discussion later in this book.

Finally, given the lower commission/bonus structure, lack of recognition and heavy workload, why would anyone want to be an SE? I believe it all boils down to risk. From a salary/commission/bonus structure, the salary and commission of an SE is typically more consistent that that received by Sales. An SE may have some high and low months, but these swings are typically not as great as they can be in Sales. We always hear about the crazy high commissions for incredibly successful Sales, but there is not a lot of talk about those months where zero commission was obtained. In addition to the more stable pay, the SE position also is more stable than the Sales position. Sales typically will have more turnover than SEs. This is usually a result of performance. Either the Sales Director elects to move on to another company or field because their pay is not reaching expectations, or the company will ask the Sales

Director to depart based on performance. This should not be shocking and is part of the Sales game. Interestingly, SEs have the ability to move within organizations quite easily while Sales Directors tend to stay in Sales. SEs have mobility into a number of disciplines such as Product, Engineering, Operations, Strategy, etc. The reason is that they must understand delivering a service from end to end and are typically engaged in all aspects of a solution. Also, obtaining knowledge about customers concerning their requirements and how they use services to further their business help to provide insight when developing products or new capabilities. Sales Directors, on the other hand, tend to stay in Sales for a lifetime. They either move up in the Sales Management ranks, or move to other companies, but functionally stay in Sales. The reason for this is that typically the pay cannot be achieved in other disciplines. So why would anyone want to be an SE? Well, there is incredible value in learning how to work directly with customers and build relationships. This helps to raise credibility with Senior Management and provides a great perspective when developing Products and capabilities. The career path becomes very open-ended by taking on the SE role for at least a few years. SE Management is a possibility, as are other fields more related to the business such as Product and Engineering (remember capital S, capital "E"). Of course, Sales is an alternative as well, but keep in mind that once you go down the Sales path, you are likely to stay in this role.

So, why not stay in Sales Engineering for a career? This is certainly an option and a good one. There are benefits to being tied into customers and revenue. This leads to more stability and provides good visibility with senior management. Further, there is typically travel involved to attend customer meetings or trade shows. As an SE, you obtain several of the benefits of Sales without performing the hard-core Sales function.

Ideal Relationship

So what is the ideal relationship between Sales and SE? In my experience, the strongest, most effective Sales/SE teams are those that act as a partnership. Each team member knows their role and trusts the other to perform. As mentioned, the Sales and SE roles are different. When teams work together to maximize the effectiveness of their roles without encroaching on each other, then the sum of the work is greater than the individual parts. Conflict can start when the SE is working on pricing or the Sales Director is developing the design. Focus on the roles and collaborate often, like every day. This is a team sport – you either close the deal or you do not (die). From an SE perspective, if you close a huge deal and the Sales Director receives a large commission, fantastic! This is part of the deal that was agreed to when accepting the role. The SE may not receive the same commission as Sales for a particular deal, but will receive the compensation that is part of the deal agreed to upon accepting the role. Again, know your role and do not let a disparity such as commission payments sour a relationship. Each team member has their own separate agreement. Know your role and focus on exceeding goals, the rest will fall into place. If you find that you are having a hard time dealing with commission disparity, then perhaps you should consider a new agreement such as taking on a Sales role.

For argument sake, let's say an SE moves into a Sales role, should they then take on the design piece of solution development? Absolutely not. If you take on the Sales role, then be the best Sales professional possible and focus on expectations and tasks for the role. You will have great insight for the tasks and expectations of the SE role, but this should performed by the SE who should be held to a high standard. Often, you may find more experienced team members partnered with junior team members. It is important for the senior members to set the bar high for the junior members to achieve. This should go both ways – Sr. Sales Director, junior SE and junior Sales Director, Sr. SE. The senior member must set the expectations. This should be based on knowledge of the role, but the person in that role needs to perform the function and "grow into it". This may be difficult at first, but the team

Show Ponies and Workhorses

will be much stronger as the junior person becomes more experienced. This will also help to scale.

Finally, the ideal Sales Team will treat their relationship as a partnership, leveraging to strengths of each team member to achieve common goals. When this occurs, the sum is greater than the parts leading to a much greater chance for success.

Chapter 4 -- Customer Relationships

Throughout the organization, the Sales Team has the unique responsibility of owning the external customer relationship. The importance of this relationship cannot be emphasized enough, as the external customer is the entity that actually agrees to pay for products or services. This is the gas in the engine. Without this agreement, you do not have a going concern no matter how well developed your products, services or processes may be. The Sales Profession is mainly focused around building customer relationships. There are several methodologies used to identify and cultivate customer relationships, typically on a commercial basis. Innumerable books, seminars, and motivational speaking engagements can be found to learn how to identify and build customer relationships. The SE will also need to identify and build relationships with the customer, but will focus on the technical personnel.

Commercial vs. Technical

The key relationships between the Sales team and the customer can be broken down into commercial and technical. Commercial relationships involve identifying key decision makers and influencers throughout the company that make purchase decisions. These are groups that may be responsible for an initiative where your product or service can be used to achieve their goal. Commercially, Sales will want to work with the person responsible for signing off on any purchase decision. Technically, the SE should identify the group or person that will approve the use of your proposed product or service. While the customer technical team does not typically sign the purchase order, nothing is usually signed unless the technical team provides their blessing. The SE role is to build a very strong relationship with the technical team typically centered on the technology. The main focus should be on capabilities and performance rather than on pricing and purchase cycles.

Value of Technical Relationships

Determine who is supportive of your company, services and the sales team. Who is rather negative and may have an agenda that does not align with your goals? Who signs the deal? Who is the most influential person at your customer to determine whether your solution is "good" or not? As an SE, one of the key relationships you must build with your customer is a great working relationship with the Technical Influencer. Understand that your role is to uncover initiatives within your customers organization that will require a technical solution that your company can provide. You must create and build relationships with key technical influencers as they are the people that will often derive the requirements and will be the key to determining whether your solution will work.

Who are technical influencers? Are they the Director of Engineering or Operations? Possibly. These individuals certainly have influence. What I am describing is the key Engineer within your customer that is going to be asked whether your solution is worth considering or buying. Often, key technical influencers do not manage teams of people, rather they are with the company due to their knowledge and past performance. While they are not featured prominently on an organization chart, these folks wield some serious technical power within the organization. As an SE, you must identify these key individuals and ideally establish a positive working relationship. You are not going to "sell" them anything. Your role is to engage them and get their input on your offerings or solutions. How in the world can you make this happen?

Engineers like to solve problems and build solutions. Also, people like to talk about themselves and what they do. How hard is it? After you identify a key technical influencer within your customer, ask a lot of questions. What sort of projects is he/she working on now? What are some of the challenges that are being experienced? If they (the influencer) were building a product or service to address some of their challenges, what would it look like? Ask the influencer if it would be OK if you ran future ideas by them "for sanity".

Technical influencers are much more likely to build a relationship if you engage them on their level and you show true respect for their knowledge and capabilities. They will often pass on an invitation to dinner or a golf outing, but have a hard time not contributing to a technical discussion on the likely roadmap for an interesting technology. Ideally, if you can receive input, suggestions and actual requirements from key influencers, you start to achieve buy-in as they become part of the solution. As you may imagine, this process is going to take some time, but this is the core activity associated with building technical relationships with your customer.

It may appear that you are working on issues and solutions for services that are a long way from reality, especially after considering the time required to traverse the product development lifecycle, but you may find incremental opportunities that can be addressed in the near term. This lays the foundation for building long term solutions with your customer. The more you can obtain input from technical influencers and incorporate these ideas into your solutions, the stronger your tie becomes. Often, this will require work within your organization to drive the ideas into products and services as requirements. This is the core function of the SE. If your relationship is strong enough, when the capabilities that your solutions provide are needed by your customer, your company is typically in the running to provide these capabilities and may be the only company offered to chance to provide that capability. This, in the Sales world is known as the "trusted advisor" zone. In the big picture, key technical influencers do not need any advisors, they need to work with an organization that understands their requirements and can be trusted to deliver a capability. Only by closely working with these individuals can you truly understand their requirements.

Understanding customer business

The best way to derive requirements is to truly understand your customer's business. How do they make money? What are the costs to providing their product or service? How much revenue can they expect? How can they run more efficiently? If you ran the company, what would you do?

These sort of questions should make you curious about your customer. Ask the question, "What if, _____?" to your technical contacts. Opening the dialog on this level leads to avenues you may not know existed. These insights can help to identify key initiatives within the company. Key initiatives are the gold found in your customer mining trips. Address these initiatives, make your contacts look good and you will see revenue. Do not view the solution for an initiative from the standpoint of what your products and services can do, rather focus on how a solution can come together to drive your customer's business. Verify that your ideas surrounding the solution are in agreement with key technical influencers and work to incorporate the requirements into any solution you develop.

Simple, right? I believe more success comes from having the proper mindset. Keeping your customer's business top of mind while respecting and incorporating key technical input from your contacts will help drive a positive relationship.

Customer Meetings and Travel

As an SE, you will often be required to travel to meet with customers or attend a conference. So why are you going on a trip? What is Sales' agenda for this trip? Should you have an agenda? To address these pithy questions, I offer the following advice:

Why are you going on travel? If you do not know, then ask some questions of your Sales team. Find out the objectives of any scheduled meeting. Sometimes just showing up at a customer location is a "check in the block" to let the customer know you still love him/her. Even if the objective is as simple as this "check in", you should build an agenda for yourself. Target your key technical contacts, set up a meeting for when you will be onsite and work to figure out how you are going to extract key initiatives from them. Travel is both expensive and necessary. Take full advantage of the opportunity to meet with your customers face to face and set your own agenda.

Setting an agenda. How do you set an agenda for your meetings? Well, what are your goals? Are there any contacts at your customer that can help you reach some of your goals? This takes critical thinking. As has been discussed, customer initiatives are the path to revenue. Your agenda should revolve around topics that will lead to a discussion of upcoming projects and initiatives. This may require setting up meetings without the Sales Director to hold a "technical check-in". Typically, you will obtain much more information from your customer contacts if the Sales Director is not present, especially if you are not viewed as "Sales". If you do have a meeting with your technical contacts, be sure to close the loop with Sales to review your findings. You should be tackling the customer as a team.

Coordinate with Sales to compare agendas and set goals for any meetings scheduled. You should have at least one goal per meeting. You may have to sit through an all-day session reviewing operational performance in exchange for a 15 minute opportunity to discuss "projects". Being able to include a discussion on projects on your meeting agenda and having a discussion on this topic is the payoff.

Chapter 5 -- Building and Maintaining Knowledge

As an SE, you must continually stay abreast of technologies and developments in your field. The reason you are part of the Sales Team is that the technology you are selling is continually evolving. You are the expert and bring value to your customers by being able to introduce or discuss new technologies that may be applicable. By being knowledgeable and establishing use cases that are directly applicable to your customers, you are laying the groundwork to have a discussion on potential projects and initiatives. Even if the use cases do not really involve your products, evaluating technology through your customer's lens differentiates you as more of an advisor than a vendor.

The "trusted advisor" concept does not just happen because you took some sales training and you learned that the top of the pyramid concerning customer interaction is the advisory role. This must be earned. You need to be able to bring something of value, such as knowledge surrounding a new or specific technology, and describe how it could be used to further your customer's business objectives. This is not a one-time deal, either. The key is to establish a relationship with influential contacts within your customer base and maintain a dialog revolving around technology and potential solutions. This will require research and imagination. It is likely that the use cases and potential solutions discussed are not even a thought from Product. But where do new Product ideas get created? Hint: Not from Product, they are fully engaged in the development and improvement of existing products and services. New ideas typically come from external sources. If you can work with your customer to brainstorm if and how a technology could be used to further business objectives, you may be able to move down the path of small-scale testing. This is where "Big E" comes into play as an SE. If you really want to move forward, you will need to take ownership of the initial phases of discovery and development. Engineering is not going to pick up your concepts and conduct the development necessary to create a new product. It is somewhat a chicken and egg problem.

Engineering and Product are not going to expend resources to develop new products unless there is a qualified business case behind it. If you can demonstrate that a new technology can be used to provide a useful service or function for your customer, then you may be able to bring the idea to start the product development lifecycle. This is not an easy task and most great ideas do not gain traction due to lack of resources, lack of interest or a marginal business case. The value in working with your customer to develop a concept that can possibly become a product is that you are working together to solve your customer's business problems. You are not selling, rather you are becoming a teammate with your customer. This provides you with multiple opportunities to meet with your customer and continue working towards key objectives. Even if you are not able to successfully bring your concept into the product development lifecycle, you build your relationship with your customer based on technical and business objectives. You start to move into an advisory role.

Running with Scissors

If you have the concept and Use Case for a new Product that aligns with your customer and believe that this is the next big thing, you will need to conduct the up front development work. Develop relationships within Engineering to see if you could possibly cobble your idea together in the lab for testing. You may need to try to obtain "demo units" of software or hardware required to use the new technology. If you are able to set up a test, you will need to develop the test plan with your customer so that you can 1) determine if the test is successful and 2) use it to argue your case that your concept should be adopted as a new product. Again, this is where "Big E" comes into play. You must use engineering principles to lay out a test plan, conduct the test and draw conclusions. You will need to use "Big S" to lay out the business case and illustrate how investing in the new technology will yield a high IRR and positive NPV.

Finally, a word of caution. If you do decide to go down a path of guerilla product development, you need to obtain support from key departments such as Engineering, Product and Finance. If your concept does not work from any of these three, it is unlikely to move forward. Ideally, you may be able to obtain buy-in from these groups to help set up a small scale test for your customer. If you can obtain the backing of your customer that they would be interested in an offering should the test be successful, then this becomes very attractive to Product as you are bringing a market to the table. Again, the concept has to work in all three areas, Engineering, Product and Finance. Championing a concept from brainstorming with your customer to entering the product development lifecycle is a long difficult path, but can payoff well. If you go down this path, you need to stick with it until you reach a conclusion. It will either be successful or fail along one or more of the three areas. The key is that you need to continue to drive the project because your credibility is tied to it. By taking ownership, you become the expert and gain tremendous knowledge of how the product or concept should work. If the concept fails, be sure to summarize your findings and explain why it is not worth pursuing to your key contacts within Engineering, Product and Finance as well as your customer. If the concept is successful, then set goals and objectives with your customer to establish timelines for delivery and work to expand the product.

Show Ponies and Workhorses

The process described could take months or years from start to finish. It is very strategic and requires an incredible effort because it will create tasks and duties above and beyond your day to day activities. The value in pursuing this process is that you begin to drive the business and differentiate yourself as a leader as well as a champion for your customer. Whether you succeed or fail, you will gain insight of your customer's business as well as your own and will need to learn the technology thoroughly. If you do decide to take this challenge, then go all in. If you do not commit, it will not be successful and may impact on your personal brand.

Chapter 6 -- Developing Expertise – Building Personal Brand

What is a personal brand? There is a lot of information concerning how to build your personal brand through the use of digital media and the ability to promote yourself. This may be how to promote a personal brand, but the bottom line is that your personal brand is how others perceive your work ethic and effectiveness. Basically, to use a playground example, when teams are being chosen for a game/sport/event you want to be one of the first picked based on your past performance. In short, your personal brand is your reputation and it is critical to develop and maintain a strong one. So what are key variables in building a personal brand? Attitude, Commitment and Drive.

Attitude

Your attitude is the one variable in which you have total control. Are you optimistic or pessimistic? Are you constantly seeing the problems that emerge or are you discovering opportunities that develop? Since you have total control over your attitude, why not choose to be positive? Like attracts like. If you are positive and believe that you can achieve goals, you will. If you are negative and do not believe that you can achieve goals, then this will occur also. That is, you will not achieve your goals. A positive, optimistic attitude is absolutely key to being successful, however you define it. It is also extremely important to truly believe in the work you are performing. How in the world are you going to sell a solution if you do not believe that it will work for your client? If you believe that the solution is not the best that you can offer or will not work, then fix it. Is there a greater opportunity with your customer if you are able to "fix" the issue? If you lose a deal, is there something to learn from your solution? Is this an opportunity? It all depends on how you view the situation.

Commitment

Are you committed to your work? Do you think about the big picture concerning how you can drive your company forward to meet objectives, or are you simply focused on how your work can benefit your career and personal objectives? Can you do better work or are you holding something back? If you are not fully committed, why? If you want to be successful and be perceived as a performer, then commit. You signed a contract to work with your current employer, so go all in. Do not get distracted by internal politics and maneuvering, focus on your job and do it well. If you find that you cannot commit to the job you are in, then you will likely need to move on. This may or may not be your choice. Set goals for yourself. Ask whether you feel that you are performing up to your standards. If it was your own company, are you putting in the same effort? If you are going to do the work, then commit. No one needs a half-assed job. If you feel that you cannot commit, then it is time to move on.

Drive

Similar to attitude, drive is totally under your control. Are you waiting for direction or are you working to set the agenda with your customers? In a Sales team environment, are you working to set the course for the technical side of the team, or are you simply reacting to strategies developed by the Sales Director? Are you challenging your team members or taking direction? You need to get your strategy into the agenda to force your customer to react. Do you set goals for yourself and do you track whether you are meeting these goals? Why push yourself? Well, it is far more interesting to be working on your own agenda that you feel is important to your success than reacting to other agendas. This can also help with time management because if you are challenging team members and other coworkers to provide information to move your projects forward, you are constantly working toward your goals. There becomes focus in your work. If you are simply waiting for direction, you are continuously reacting to others, typically through email which may be blocking you from working on your goals. Be a driver not a passenger.

Show Ponies and Workhorses

All three of these variables are within your control as mentioned. How you choose to implement them will define your personal brand. It's not how you promote yourself, rather how others perceive you. Your brand is even more influenced on how you perform and act when others are not looking. This is your true brand that it will come through in your actions.

Your personal brand will be on display at customer meetings, presentations you deliver, meetings you run and through your internal communication and coordination. In any of these situations, you are showcasing your talents and providing a data point for others to develop a perception. How do you want to be perceived? Professional, prepared, technically astute? If so, you must provide this perception, EVERY TIME. There are no "passes" on these activities. Your preparation should be thorough for each instance and you should prepare the same way every time so that when you do not prepare going into a meeting or providing a presentation, you should feel that you are "missing something". This is why checklists are used in aviation. The process should be so rote that when you miss a step, something feels wrong. Develop a checklist for your preparation. An example checklist for customer meetings may include:

- Meeting Agenda
- Meeting Goal

- Define Next Steps

When providing presentations, a reasonable checklist includes:

- Define the Audience
- Storyboard your message
- What is the key point?
- Identify and address likely questions and feedback
- Is the focus of your presentation on the speaker? Is it visually interesting?
- Did you rehearse the presentation?

Finally, for internal communication, be respectful and provide supporting information for any issue requiring your input. At times internal organizations have conflict, sometimes this is by design so that the organization becomes more competitive. Do not confuse organizational conflict with personal attacks. After all, everyone is on the same team within a company or organization. Even if there are personal conflicts, stay professional and remain true to your personal brand. How you react to conflict can greatly influence perceptions of you. If you provide supporting data with your statements, especially when working on an issue with conflicting opinions, you at least are providing a defendable argument. This may take research, but is worth the supporting information and adds to your personal brand. Do not respond immediately to inflammatory emails, rather take time to craft a response with supporting information of your viewpoint.

One last point to keep in mind is that typically everyone in an organization is looking to perform their best. Many are dedicated to the work that they perform and when an obstacle is reached, there is typically energy expended to remove the obstacle. Your work may be an obstacle to the completion of other groups tasks or goals. Your work then becomes the focus of the energy to remove the obstacle. Keep in mind that you personally are not the focus, but rather the work or task you are performing are. There may be very good reasons why your work is preventing another group from proceeding, of course, there also could be no reason why your work is preventing progress either. The key is to collaborate with the teams or groups affected by the conflict and view the situation objectively. Respond to any conflict according to your personal brand and understand that no employee is always right, including yourself.

Process

Be a student of the processes your organization uses to "get things done". This could be the Sales Process or the Custom Build process or how funding is allocated to projects. Sometimes the process is a mess. If you find this situation, work to improve the process. The key in any situation, however, is to understand what the existing process is. Right or wrong, the existing process is what is used to complete work. If your order process has 47 steps in it, learn them all and figure out how to move through them efficiently. Hopefully, this is not the case, but the point is that you can only move the ball forward if you follow the process. If there is a better way, then figure out who can help you to make changes and work to improve the process.

The work of the SE is all about revenue. The key process is the sales order process and this needs to be as efficient as possible. When developing solutions, keep in mind the time it will take to implement a solution. Does the solution fall within a standard offering that can fit neatly into a defined process? If so, the time to implement should be well documented and expectations can be set with your customer. If the customer is asking for "special features", the question should be what the impact of the request is on revenue. If the request requires engineering work that falls outside of the process, it will take longer to implement. How much longer? What is the revenue impact of this delay? Is this revenue impact greater than the opportunity presented by the request? Is the work required to implement the customer request impacting your ability to address solutions for other customers?

Just because a customer has a request, this does not mean that they will shower your company with revenue for implementing the request. Have you exhausted all efforts using standard products and services? Will the request lead to a new service or product that can be sold to multiple customers and drive revenue or is it a one-off for the customer? If it is a one-off, how much revenue will it drive compared to what they already spend? If you do not take on the request, is there an impact to existing revenue with the customer? One of the most difficult discussions that can occur with a Sales Director is to convince them that it is not worth pursuing a customer request that leads to a custom solution. An impact analysis should be performed along the lines of "standard" vs. "non-standard" products or services. Often, accepting non-standard requests results in more account management to deal with the problems associated with the non-standard offering resulting in less time to capture revenue from other customers.

Learn the process and "stick with the script" concerning what your company offers. The goal is not to develop custom solutions that address every customer nuance, rather it is to address customer requirements as efficiently as possible with the existing toolset. This may sound unimaginative, but the real trick is to learn how to present the tradeoffs of the benefit of going with standard products and services in exchange for higher availability and faster implementation. The SE should not be developing new products and services, instead the focus should be on selling what is offered and minimizing time to revenue.

Technology

Become an expert in one or more of the key technologies you sell. As an SE, you will be viewed as the key technical contributor for your company with your customer. Know your products and services down to the theoretical level. Stay abreast of new developments and technologies and be ready to discuss with key engineering and technical contacts at your customer. Your level of understanding should be such that you are comfortable presenting it at a conference full of peered technical talent. This avoids the statement often heard during customer meetings, "I will follow up with you on that question." Do not be that SE, rather, be the SE that takes the bull by the horns to not only address the question, but furthers the conversation by digging into the details and pushing the customer for more details concerning why they are asking. With knowledge comes confidence. To be an equal member of the Sales team, you have to earn your spot with your technical knowledge and ability to make your customer react. This brings value to the team.

Communication

It is essential to establish a great working relationship between Sales and SE. Typically, an SE is assigned to one or more Sales

Directors. To work as a team, Sales and SE must communicate daily. Aligning agendas can be straightforward if an SE is only assigned to one Sales Director, but when an SE is assigned to multiple Sales Directors, priority conflicts can occur. An effective way to assign priority is through ranking priorities by revenue. Of course, every situation is different where all the variables need to be considered. The one constant for successfully resolving priority conflicts is establishing and maintaining excellent communication with all members of your team. Lay out your priorities and schedule with your Sales Directors, discuss areas of conflict and ask for feedback on how best to resolve. Opening lines of communication with Sales Management is also an excellent idea. Work to understand the departmental goals and how your Sales Director fits into the plan. Align your goals with the Sales goals, both individual and departmental. Finally, when conflicts and issues arise, overcommunicate. Provide updates to all affected parties and not only report on the issue, but also offer the leading solution to resolve.

Communication is also paramount when working with customers. Often, the SE will get pulled into Operational issues or delays in deployment because the Sales team is typically the customer interface. When addressing issues or problems with the customer, communicate the situation with integrity and work to have a path toward resolution before contacting the customer. In many instances, the customer may be disappointed or upset and will likely offer criticism. Maintaining your personal brand, listen to the customer in these situations, allow them to vent if necessary. Do not offer excuses or try to explain why an event happened. Provide the information you have objectively, explain your next steps and schedule a time to follow up. As a customer facing professional, being the interface for issues is one of the more difficult tasks. When you do follow up, be sure to have all the data surrounding the event and the path to resolution. This is often an opportunity to get information out of your customer concerning their initiatives or business to understand why there was such an impact. Sometimes if the customer overreacts to a situation, they feel somewhat guilty which can be beneficial on the follow up call. It does not happen every time, but be aware of a window of opportunity should you experience this situation.

Common sense dictates that maintaining constant communication with team members and customers is a good practice. Establish this by informally calling or touching base with key contacts and teammates. A simple five-minute check in call on a regular basis really helps to maintain relationships and avoid surprises. Finally, it is always more pleasant to communicate with those that you like. It is strongly encouraged

Show Ponies and Workhorses

to build relationships on both the personal and professional level and build a positive environment.

Chapter 7 -- Time Management

Multitasking

Have you ever heard the mantra, "My job requires me to multitask", or "I am a great multitasker"? There seems to be a badge of honor within our society that holds the "multitasker" in great esteem and places them on a high pedestal. I am telling you that this is complete nonsense. In the Sales Engineering environment, you will accumulate more tasks than can be done in a day, week or month. In other words, you will always have more tasks to complete than can be completed. So, how should this be tackled?

The first answer that may come to mind is to simply "hire more people", that way the load will be spread among a larger group and the workload will be more manageable. Here's the secret, the workload is never going to stop, or get more "manageable". No manager worth his/her salt is going to ask for more headcount without a good business case. This typically gets down to the Sales to SE ratio that is typical for your company. I have seen the ratio as low as 1:1 for extremely technical sales and much higher for transactional type sales. Whatever the ratio, the SE workload will always be "high". So, adding headcount typically means that the Sales team is expanding. If the Sales team is expanding, then new Sales personnel will need to be trained on the product or service being offered, and who is going to show them the ropes?

So, then the answer must be multitasking, right? I believe that the concept of multitasking has been elevated to a desirable trait by early adopters of technology such as millennials while in their college years so that society provides an acceptance of this behavior. This acceptance then allows students or workers to then distract themselves with personal, irrelevant information, typically found through smartphones and social media while "on the job". When confronted about their decline in productivity, multitaskers will use the defense that they have grown up with technology and have multitasked their entire lives claiming that their generation has this mystical capability and older generations simply "Do not get it". Of course, this is all bullshit.

I have taught "Digital Media and Society" at the University of Maryland, University College for over five years. Every class includes a discussion on multitasking after reviewing a fantastic documentary from PBS Frontline (http://www.pbs.org/wgbh/frontline/film/digitalnation/). In the first part of the documentary, Professor Turkle of MIT illustrates the problem of multitasking with her students. I have had this discussion with hundreds of college students, and there is a trend among the younger students that believe they can multitask because somehow they were either born with this trait or their use of smartphones has genetically altered them for this capability. Of course, this is not true, but the sad thing is that society is accepting of this behavior. I am not going to be able to reverse this trend, but I can suggest how you can set yourself apart from the crowd on your performance by not falling into this trap.

Stanford University has also conducted a study on multi-tasking (http://news.stanford.edu/2009/08/24/multitask-research-study-082409/) finding that humans do not have the ability to actually multitask like a multi-processor computer and perform mediocre at all the activities while multitasking. The subjects of the experiments show that high multitaskers cannot help but be distracted, resulting in lower performance of the task at hand, even after explicit instruction to ignore certain objects. Humans tend to switch between tasks when "multitasking" and that it takes time to refocus every time a switch is made. So if you are trying to multitask between two tasks, the "switching time" required will cause the time to complete both tasks to be longer and the performance will be worse for both tasks. If you try to multitask between three tasks, the results will be even worse.

So what is the answer? Two things: Prioritization and Focus.

Prioritization

Prioritization is Time Management 101. If you have more tasks to complete than can be accomplished in a period of time, then the answer is to rank the importance of completing the tasks in order and focus on each task until it is completed. Note that this means you should place laser focus on the task at hand and complete it before moving onto the next task. If the task requires more time to complete than you can allocate to it, set a goal to complete a portion of the task within the allotted time period and work until you hit your goal. If you prioritize your tasks, but "multitask" across two or more tasks, you not only will increase the amount of time required to complete all the tasks but you will make up for it by generating sub-par work. You will also feel more stressed when multitasking, as you should because your work will not be your best.

One of the highest hurdles I have faced while being an SE is learning how to manage my own schedule. Trust me, everyone has their own agenda, particularly Sales. Your colleagues will look to schedule meetings to serve their agenda, but this may not be the best use of your time. How do you avoid being scheduled for a meeting when you are planning to complete work on a project? Schedule time to complete a task on your calendar and call it a project meeting. The meeting will have one attendee –you, and the agenda is the completion of your task or goal. Take control of your schedule! Schedule blocks of time to complete tasks. The important thing is that when the meeting time arrives, you need to minimize the email, silence your phone and focus on completing the task at hand. When the scheduled time is up, then shut down work on the task, re-engage on email and turn up the volume on your phone. In other words, create a focused session to complete work and during this time, dedicate yourself to completing the task you have scheduled. Treat this time like you are meeting with an important customer, give it the prioritization and focus it deserves.

So how should tasks be prioritized? The easiest, most effective measurement to use for prioritization is revenue. That is, how does the task at hand drive revenue and how much is it driving? As an SE, your role is to drive revenue. If you are working to determine the level of priority between similar customer requests, which one is tied to bringing in new or more revenue? The highest wins. Often, customer requests revolve around Operational issues on products or services that have already been sold. You can get completely absorbed by these sort of requests that generate absolutely no additional revenue. These sorts of issues have got to be handed off to either Customer Service or Operations, your role is to drive revenue. Why is revenue such an important metric? Because this is what drives

Sales and they are hard pressed to argue against your logic. Keep in mind that prioritization is only setting the order for tasks that you work. It does not recuse you from actually completing all the tasks on your list. So, if there is conflict in your prioritization, then change it if you need to and complete one task over the other. The point is to have a model to use when things get overwhelming. Prioritization and focus will present a path through the chaos.

Agenda

Everyone has an agenda. Some are more important than others, but everyone has them. Often, we go along with agendas by attending meetings that we really do not understand why we are invited or tracking down information that is requested through email. It can become very easy to be driven by these agendas to the point where the entire business day is spent reacting and not driving forward with your goals. The key is to define whether a requested action is in alignment with YOUR agenda or not. Wouldn't it be nice to spend most of your time accomplishing your goals? With so many meetings and a constant flow of email, how can the distractions be eliminated? You need to create your agenda.

The first step is to clearly define your role and your responsibilities. In an organization, there are several tasks that must be performed. Every employee needs to play their position. If you are playing other positions, you are creating gaps with your own position. Once you have your position defined, then create goals to achieve. These must be true goals that have specific, measurable results to be accomplished within a given timeframe. Everyone has annual performance management goals that are typically assigned by management. The goals you create could be part of the annual performance management goals, but should be for shorter timeframes such as a day or week. These are the incremental steps towards achieving a larger goal. At the start of each day, write down the goals you plan to achieve that day or possibly that week. Do this before you start the email treadmill. Make a habit of revisiting your goals by scratching off the ones you complete and keeping the goals that you have not yet completed. Keep the goals until they are completed. These goals become YOUR agenda.

Once you have established your agenda, set up meetings to obtain information or help to meet your goals or send emails to those that may be able to help you complete your goals. If you receive meeting requests that are not aligned with your goals or your customers, then decline them. Focus on your goals. If you receive emails that are not immediately related to your goals and customers, move on. Do not spend time reading emails copied to half of the company. We all have a position to play,

Show Ponies and Workhorses

focus your efforts on your position and try to minimize the chatter and activity outside of your role.

Chapter 8 -- Issues and Resolution

As with any role in an organization, there will be issues. The role of the SE is a central one that often bridges between Sales, Product, Engineering and even Finance. The following are some common issues that you may experience along with some advice on how to deal with them. In general, the most effective way to overcome issues is to constantly communicate with all your contacts and interfaces.

The Difficult Sales Director

In a career, it is inevitable that you will get paired or teamed with a Sales Director that is not in alignment with the way you work or your goals. For example, you may set a tone of preparation for any meeting outlining specific goals and developing agendas. Some Sales Directors seem to "wing it", schedule meetings without your knowledge, then pull you into the meeting as an afterthought with no time for you to prepare. This situation requires some one-on-one communication. Whether you get along or not, you must perform as a team. It is important to establish how you expect to work with your customers and to come to agreement on your goals. Typically, your goals should be aligned around revenue. If you want to prepare for meetings, you need to be given enough time prior to any meeting to do so. You may also drive the need to establish an agenda and goal for each meeting that both of you are responsible for creating.

The dynamic can be very difficult for new SEs to the company paired with established Sales Directors. There may be several years of experience difference between the two and the Sales Director may be very successful. In these cases, it will be helpful to meet with other SEs that have worked with a Sales Director to understand how he/she works. The important item to convey to the Sales Director is that you want to be considered a team member responsible for the technical lead on the account and not the Sales Director's "bitch". An SE is not the Sales Director's admin or assistant, although they may be viewed that way if the SE allows it. Do not fall into this trap. I highly recommend working with experienced SEs and SE Management on strategies how to build your reputation or personal brand as a team member and provide value to the team.

The bottom line is that the role of the SE is a discipline by itself. The SE must be able to work creatively, build relationships and drive customers technically. If the relationship with Sales is one where the SE is constantly reacting to Sales requests, the SE will not be as effective which will only harm the performance of the team. It is important for the SE to establish their role on the Sales team to allow for independence and creativity. In new team assignments, this may or may not happen immediately depending on the skill and experience of both Sales and SE. For newer SEs, this may be an iterative process through a series of "proving" themselves.

Organizational Power

It is imperative to understand which teams wield "the power" in an organization. Is the company "Sales Driven" or "Product Driven"? Typically, all groups have some form of influence over the others, but in general, the group that seems to get their way the most has the "power". Often, customers will request non-standard capabilities resulting in a "one-off" design to address their requirements. How does the organization react to this request? Let's use the following scenario and company reaction to determine where the power lies.

Scenario: A vendor has developed a new capability to virtualize services through the deployment of gear produced by the vendor running a proprietary protocol. Your customer wants to leverage the new capability offered by the new gear to reduce their operational cost and run your services over the new gear. Your customer is looking for your company to deploy and manage the new gear and offer a new service to them.

Product Driven Response: Business cases are required to prove that the cost of deployment of the new gear will be offset by the customer commitment and potential forecast for other customers to use. The new gear will need to be vetted by Engineering for performance testing. The new gear will enter a product development lifecycle so that it can be ordered, properly deployed by Operations and maintained by the NOC. The timeframe for deployment is likely to be from 6 months to 2 years and will result in a new product that can be offered to both your customer and their competitors.

Sales Driven Response: A business case will be run for the specific deal with your customer to prove that the revenue on the deal will pay for the new gear. A trial will be set up to deploy the new gear according to the customer specific requirements. The operational and engineering details will be worked out as the trial progresses. The implementation will occur in 1-2 months.

For Product driven companies, standard process and design have high regard. The customer request in the scenario above may be a great idea and opportunity, but will need to go through the product development lifecycle process in order to actually be offered to the customer. The incremental revenue offered by the customer does not outweigh the need to operate within established processes.

For Sales driven companies, revenue has high regard. The customer request is viewed as an opportunity that can be expanded to include similar customers. The company likely has numerous custom designs and a handful of standard products. Deployment of solutions requires effort from many organizations but the incremental revenue and potential revenue is worth the non-standard deployment.

It is important to understand where the power lies in your company, as the response to customer requests can be vastly different. It does not matter which way you feel is better, it does matter how your company reacts. If you are trying to develop solutions that are the opposite of your company's viewpoint, you will not be in alignment and will have internal friction. You will not be able to change the company viewpoint from one to the other, this only can happen through a major reorganization of processes. Of course, companies are not 100% Product or 100% Sales, there is usually some mix of the two. In a Sales driven environment, you will need to develop what works in the near term and be open to a variety of customer requests. In a Product driven environment, you will want to capture customer requests as requirements and bring to Product for review. In any case, you need to respond to your customer with the likely action. Understand if your company is Product or Sales driven and act accordingly.

Competing Priorities

The SE role is busy. Typically, there is more to do than can be done in a day, so how can the work be completed? The key is setting priorities. As has been mentioned, revenue should have an oversized influence on your priorities as revenue should be the key metric for an SE. Align tasks in decreasing order of revenue, then by due date. Sometimes there needs to be negotiation on due dates with both the customer and the Sales Team. Be able to document your tasks and priorities to provide the reason for their order. In general, Sales seems to rely on one tool more than others to resolve conflict. That tool is escalation. Do not be surprised if your Sales Director, your teammate, escalates to your manager that you are not doing your job. This is usually the result of a discussion you have with the Sales Director indicating that you will need to extend a deadline for a deliverable due to competing priorities. This is where your list of priorities comes into play. If you can clearly show your priorities and how they align with revenue, you have given your manager enough information to make a decision on your priority list. Your manager may agree with your list and work out the deadline with Sales and may even pull in additional resources to help, or may change your priorities.

To reiterate, communication is key in both your internal and external relationships. If you have competing priorities across multiple Sales Directors that force conflict in due dates, then I highly recommend briefing your manager with the conflict. When you present the issue, be sure to also present your solution. This action solves two problems; it keeps your manager up to date on a potential issue, and basically serves as defense against escalation. If a Sales Director does escalate, do not take it personally as hard as this may be. Maintain your personal brand, and do not retaliate. You may want to discuss the situation with your Sales Director and try to work similar issues out in the future. Work to identify the conflict before it becomes an issue and ask for help from management. This will typically yield a better result.

Work Overload

Often, competing priorities can lead to work overload. Workload seems to come in waves where there are times of overactivity followed by more reasonable demand loads. Again, involving management is key in these situations. Management can help offload some work by applying more resources, and serve as a buffer for escalations. There is a fine line to learn between simply "getting it done" and raising an issue with management. Reaching out for help with management too much does not reflect well on your ability to handle the role, but never reaching out in overload situations can lead to burn out. If you have one-on-one meetings with management, be sure to include workload as a topic for each session. That way you consistently address the topic and you are able to receive help when needed.

Unrealistic Expectations

One of the most maddening situations occurs when others set unrealistic expectations for delivery of your work. This can be overcome when working with external customers by attending most of the meetings with them. It is important to set proper expectations especially when conveying delivery times. The adage, "under promise and overdeliver", is a good rule to follow. Give yourself a time buffer for contingencies and delays. Also, if you set a date for delivery, do not promise the last day of the month, rather promise the first day of the following month. If you miss the former promise by one day, you miss the date by a month in the customer's eyes. If you miss the delivery by one day on the latter example, you only miss by a day.

To keep your sales team on the same page, provide delivery timeframes for common deliverables. These could be designs, circuit deliveries, gear installations, etc. If unrealistic expectations are set with the customer or internal organizations, communicate directly and reset expectations. It is far better to address the error as close to when the expectation was delivered than after the "due date" has passed.

The Difficult Customer

What company does not have one of these? The more revenue received from a particular customer, the more demanding they become. This is because a customer becomes dependent on your services for their business. While you may not be partners as in a joint venture, you certainly are working together to achieve business goals. If you are on the account for a "hot list" or "key account" customer, you have some tradeoffs. The good side of the equation is that these customers typically purchase services on a consistent basis. The other side of the equation is that high delivery expectations are set. For high-value, difficult customers, it is important to establish key technical relationships. The SE can be instrumental in the overall relationship with the customer because if the technical issues can be resolved at the working level, escalation may be avoided to senior levels. Escalations tend to animate senior management which results in the assignment of work with the customer. So basically, you need to control your destiny by reaching out to the customer and being proactive to learn about issues and initiatives, or you may be directed to resolve issues as part of a "fire drill".

Amazingly, some low-value customers that like to escalate tend to get some of the same treatment as high-value customers simply because senior management gets animated. Again, the

Show Ponies and Workhorses

strategy should be to establish strong relationships with these customers at the engineering and ops level. This will help to explain why an escalation is taking place and helps to level set the response from senior management.

Chapter 9 -- Why I was an SE

The SE is an essential component of the Sales Team and is often thought of as the "glue" between Sales and key departments within an organization such as Engineering, Product, Operations and Finance. The experience gained in the position of SE provides knowledge of how the company actually works and provides a foundation to work in virtually any aspect of the business, including Sales. Some professionals have an inclination to build customer relationships, push opportunities and focus on closing deals. Others may be attracted to Sales, but may not have the inclination to push opportunities or close deals. It is extremely valuable to understand how Sales works whether you are on the sell side or the buy side. Performing on a Sales team provides key insight on the purchase process and can aide in a variety of positions, especially in management where buying decisions are made. Further, the work of the SE is highly visible to management, especially when working on key accounts. This visibility can lead to leadership opportunities within and outside of the company. Of course, the SE role also has management opportunity and is a good career path on its own. It is an excellent blend of business and technical acumen and is both challenging and rewarding. Finally, an SE has direct impact on the performance of a company and its ability to drive revenue.

Final Thoughts

Whether you are new to the role of SE, or a wily veteran, there is always something new to learn, especially in technology. The best advice I can provide to any SE is to be strong. Know what you bring to the table on your team and firmly grasp the responsibility as technical lead. If new products or technologies are developed that have direct relevance to your solutions, then do what it takes to become an expert on the technology. Continue to be a student of the process within your own organization and learn how to drive your solutions through to acceptance internally. Above all, be bold, confident and positive. Treat yourself as an equal member of the Sales team. This will demand others to do the same. Hold your teammates and other departments within your organization accountable for their deliverables to you. Assign tasks to others that are in position to help you to achieve your goals. Deliver what you say you will, better yet, overdeliver what you say you will. Prioritize and focus on the goals you set for yourself. Finally, visualize your success and it will fall into place. Go ahead, be the "workhorse" you know you are.

Works Cited

Merriam-Webster Online Dictionary. (2017, May 2). Retrieved from Merriam-webster.com: https://www.merriam-webster.com/dictionary/engineer

Our Concept and Definition of Critical Thinking. (2017, May 05). Retrieved from The Critical Thinking Community: http://www.criticalthinking.org/pages/our-concept-and-definition-of-critical-thinking/411

www.ingramcontent.com/pod-product-compliance
Lightning Source LLC
Chambersburg PA
CBHW030443220526
45464CB00006B/2400